MAMA WHAT'S THAT ON YOUR FACE?

WRITTEN & ILLUSTRATED BY
MICHELE GMITROWSKI

Copyright © 2020 Michele Gmitrowski.

Cover and Interior design by Michele Gmitrowski

This is a short story children's book

All rights reserved.

No part of this book may be reproduced or used in any manner without written permission of the copyright owner except for the use of quotations in a book review.

This book is dedicated
to all my grandchildren
you all gave me the inspiration to write my
very first children's book.

Thank you,
Love, Nana

Mama what's that on your Face?

I cannot see your smile...

Are you happy or are you sad?

Do you have to wear it every place?

Son, it is called a Mask

When I take it off I am happy, can you see?

There is no need to be afraid of me.

But Mama I don't understand

It is scary for me...

Why do you have to wear that?

Can I touch it with my hand?

Well let me tell you son...

There is a nasty thing called COVID, it is a virus that can make you sick.

What I am wearing on my face is a mask

But Mama I don't want you to get sick

Not even a little bit...

Please take it off Mama
so I can see you smile

When we are out I have to wear it

To protect you and me

I know it's hard to understand

But when we get home you will see

Now that we are home I will try to explain

Sit down my son and I will go through all of it again

This nasty thing called COVID
it is so very bad.
It spreads in so many places
And make so many people sad
As you see when people cough or sneeze
They don't always cover their mouth...

So all the germs go everywhere
It's feels like a breeze
But this breeze does not feel good
It spreads bad germs that can make
this virus spread

Mama, will it hurt me?
Tell me what to do

Son, like Mama, you have to protect yourself

And wear a mask too.

Don't be scared son,

I will keep COVID away...

I will protect you son

So you can still have fun and play

But Mama t do I have to wear a mask

And when can I go out and play

Son you cannot be with many friends

Well, at least not today.

When that monster, COVID finally goes away, we still have to be careful son just like we are today. But until then, we have to do these things. Wash our hands wear a mask and practice. Something called social distancing

Mama what is social distancing?

I stand here and you stand there. You see we are apart. When we do this it keeps us safe. Right from the very start. So if we do all this then we can all say.

Hey! COVID Monster, please stay away?

Thank you Mama for telling me, so I won't be so scared. It's so nice to have a Mama who shows she really cares.

About the Author

Michele Gmitrowski was born in Calcutta, India, but raised in the United Kingdom from the age of four. When she was sixteen, she and her family immigrated to Canada, where she still lives today. Her heritage is a mixture of Spanish, Irish, Armenian, and British. As a child, Ms. Gmitrowski was a tomboy-always playing soldiers with the neighborhood kids, and loving to write detective stories as a pastime. As she grew older, she became a lover of poems, and eventually had one of her own published in 2004, in VoicesNet Anthology. She also had a book published in 2019, The Darkness Within by Inkwater Press, her memoir, And a Mystery Thriller, Seduced By a Predator by Inkwater Press/Ingramsparks in 2020.

Michele Gmitrowski was born in Calcutta, India, but raised in the United Kingdom from the age of four. When she was sixteen, she and her family immigrated to Canada, where she still lives today. Her heritage is a mixture of Spanish, Irish, Armenian, and British. As a child, Ms. Gmitrowski was a tomboy-always playing soldiers with the neighborhood kids, and loving to write detective stories as a pastime. As she grew older, she became a lover of poems, and eventually had one of her own published in 2004, in VoicesNet Anthology. She also had a book published in 2019, The Darkness Within by Inkwater Press, her memoir And a Mystery Thriller, Seduced By a Predator by Inkwater Press/Ingramsparks in 2020. Ms Gmitrowski is happily married and has two wonderful children (a son and a daughter), as well as four grandchildren. Her family makes her feel quite blessed.

www.ingramcontent.com/pod-product-compliance
Lightning Source LLC
Chambersburg PA
CBHW051306110526
44589CB00025B/2952